A Coast of Trees

A Coast of Trees

Poems

••

A. R. AMMONS

W · W · NORTON & COMPANY

NEW YORK   LONDON

9/1981
am. Lit.

Copyright © 1981 by A. R. Ammons
Published simultaneously in Canada by George J. McLeod Limited, Toronto.
Printed in the United States of America
All Rights Reserved
First Edition

Library of Congress Cataloging in Publication Data
Ammons, A   R   1926–
A coast of trees. Poems.
I. Title.
PS3501.M6C57   1981   811'.54   80–19973
ISBN 0–393–01447–9
ISBN 0–393–00051–6 (pbk.)

W. W. Norton & Company, Inc. 500 Fifth Avenue, New York, N.Y. 10110
W. W. Norton & Company Ltd. 25 New Street Square, London EC4A 3NT
1 2 3 4 5 6 7 8 9 0

for Phyllis

Contents

Acknowledgments

The following poems first appeared in and by these periodicals and presses:

The Hudson Review—Weather-Bound, Density, Vehicle, Response, Distraction, Rapids, Night Finding, Sunday at McDonald's, Feel Like Traveling On, Poverty;

American Poetry Review—In Memoriam Mae Noblitt, Keepsake, Dry Spell Spiel, Givings, An Improvisation for the Stately Dwelling, An Improvisation for Jerald Bullis;

Poetry—Strolls, Getting Through (formerly, The Brook has Worked out the Prominences of a Bend), Easter Morning, Persistences;

The Hampden-Sydney Review—Antithesis, Range, Sweetened Change;

Rainy Day—Coast of Trees, Where;

The Beloit Poetry Journal—Eventually Is Soon Enough (formerly, Warming Trend);

Diacritics—Mountain Wind;

The Iowa Review—Continuing;

Laurel Review—Parting (formerly, Parting Lovers);

The Michigan Review—Country Music;

The Ohio Review—Swells;

Palaemon Press—Breaking Out;

The Poetry Miscellany—Traveling Shows;

Southern Poetry Review—Neighbors.

A Coast of Trees

Coast of Trees

The reality is, though susceptible
to versions, without denomination:
when the fences foregather
the reality they shut in is cast out:
if the name nearest the name
names least or names
only a verge before the void takes naming in,
how are we to find holiness,
our engines of declaration put aside,
helplessness our first offer and sacrifice,
except that having given up all mechanisms of
approach, having accepted a shambles of
non-enterprise, we know a unity
approach divided, a composure past
sight: then, with nothing, we turn
to the cleared particular, not more
nor less than itself, and we realize
that whatever it is it is in the Way and
the Way in it, as in us, emptied full.

Swells

The very longest swell in the ocean, I suspect,
carries the deepest memory, the information of actions
summarized (surface peaks and dibbles and local sharp

slopes of windstorms) with a summary of the summaries
and under other summaries a deeper summary: well, maybe
deeper, longer for length here is the same as deep

time: so that the longest swell swells least; that
is, its effects in immediate events are least perceptible,
a pitch to white water rising say a millimeter more

because of an old invisible presence: and on the ocean
floor an average so vast occurs it moves in a noticeability
of a thousand years, every blip, though, of surface and

intermediacy moderated into account: I like to go
to old places where the effect dwells, summits or seas
so hard to summon into mind, even with the natural

ones hard to climb or weigh: I go there in my mind
(which is, after all, where these things negotiably are)
and tune in to the wave nearly beyond rise or fall in its

staying and hum the constant, universal assimilation: the
information, so packed, nearly silenced with majesty
and communicating hardly any action: go there and

rest from the ragged and rapid pulse, the immediate threat
shot up in a disintegrating spray, the many thoughts and
sights unmanageable, the deaths of so many, hungry or mad.

Continuing

Considering the show, some prize-winning
leaves broad and firm, a good year,
I checked the ground
for the accumulation of
fifty seasons: last year was
prominent to notice, whole leaves
curled, some still with color:
and, underneath, the year
before, though paler, had structure,
partial, airier than linen:
but under that,
sand or rocksoil already mixed
with the meal or grist:
is this, I said to the mountain,
what becomes of things:
well, the mountain said, one
mourns the dead but who
can mourn those the dead mourned;
back a way
they sift in a tearless
place: but, I said,
it's so quick, don't you think,
quick: most time, the mountain said, lies
in the thinnest layer: who
could bear to hear of it:

I scooped up the sand which flowed
away, all but a cone in the palm:
the mountain said, it
will do for another year.

In Memoriam
Mae Noblitt

This is just a place:
we go around, distanced,
yearly in a star's

atmosphere, turning
daily into and out of
direct light and

slanting through the
quadrant seasons: deep
space begins at our

heels, nearly rousing
us loose: we look up
or out so high, sight's

silk almost draws us away:
this is just a place:
currents worry themselves

coiled and free in airs
and oceans: water picks
up mineral shadow and

plasm into billions of
designs, frames: trees,
grains, bacteria: but

is love a reality we
made here ourselves—
and grief—did we design

that—or do these,
like currents, whine
in and out among us merely

as we arrive and go:
this is just a place:
the reality we agree with,

that agrees with us,
outbounding this, arrives
to touch, joining with

us from far away:
our home which defines
us is elsewhere but not

so far away we have
forgotten it:
this is just a place.

Weather-Bound

A strong southwester
brings up the south
and our moths having been
already under snow
and freezing air
waken and search for
prominences, pebbles, straw tips,
to flutter away from:
but they want to go where
the wind is coming from:
they lift off and the
wind blusters them high:
they flutter hard
but glance away to the
right or left or
fly backward forward:
maybe they really want
to go north
but must do so into the wind
or tumble wind-fraught
against tearing shrubs:
overnight a shower barely wetting
settles them out of the air again
and seals their wings
to macadam and concrete:

surface tension sets in
like gangrene
and their dust softens, mud:
this takes fluttering
and destination out of them:
they sit
like aircraft, headed south,
their minds as if not
on the controls or removed.

Where

Where are the shifts
of the tide kept, so many:
(where are they put away) and
the wind's changes:

when glaciers breaking
down gaps
crawl through, where
are the windings saved:

wiggles of brook worms, earworms,
flickers of fire on
timber or walls or
(lostly) stars—shades of

actions, where are they:
there where motions
are stilled, stored, rehearsed,
recalled, there, there!

Strolls

The brook gives me
sparkles plenty, an
abundance, but asks
nothing of me:
snow thickets
and scrawny
snowwork of hedgerows,
still gold weeds, and
snow-bent cedar gatherings
provide
feasts of disposition
(figure, color, weight, proportion)
and require
not even that I notice:
the near-winter quartermoon
sliding high almost
into color at four-thirty—
the abundance of clarity
along the rose ridge line!
alone, I'm not alone:
a standoffishness and reasonableness
in things finds
me or I find that
in them: sand, falls,

furrow, bluff—
things one, speaking things
not words, would
have found to say.

Getting Through

The brook has worked
out the prominences of
a bend so as to find
curvature's sliding
speed and now thaw
or shower can reach it
to shell the shale out
from an overhung ledge:
the ledge bends way
over as if to contemplate
its solution in a spill:
right now I think
the skinny old arborvita's
roots may be holding everything
together: but when the spill
comes the brook will have
another heap
in its way, another
shambles to get
through or around: or
over: how much times does
a brook have: how much
time a brook has!

Eventually Is
Soon Enough

Lee of wind-skinned rises
long drifts of
fallout snow soak in the thaw:
the brook, the sky bright
for days, steps lightly
down ledge steps:
anything black enough
to be furrow soil will turn
out to be old snow bank,
trickling:
snowplows plowed snow
into shrubrows that give
reservoir humped mesh:
thickets that paused a lot
out of the air
streak it with chilling shade,
cold huddling, keep
flood from falling,
give away a little at a
time longer than
roofs and slanty, beam-turned banks do:
this soundless (no rain or
thunder) upstirring of

the brook!
the mediations and mixtures,
flows and pauses: one sees on the bank
of a cleared ditch
swatches of ground moss so green
one thinks with relief
spring won't have to improve any on that.

Density

A bluejay's the clarified
bush's only ornament:
except for two or three
tan-fine leaves he
rattles on a twig:
and there's where summer's
hidden trickle
got its tune, the end of
a corrugated pipe
undercrossing the road:
and down there
farther where density
hid all but the hermit
lark's song
is a gang of wires, once
woodvine: winter
putting so much
away leaves too
much room to see.

Vehicle

I take myself, in
the goal of my destiny,
the way the wind takes
me, something to
stir, run, and dismiss,
or the way dust
or falling snow take
me (obstruction,
scaffolding) a form
of delay—that is,
nothing to nothing:
but meanwhile my
body knows the wind and
calls it out,
and dust and snow,
the running brook,
praise themselves seen in
my praising sight.

Response

Fuzzy baby-spider ball
hanging in the spirea bush,
the harder the wind blew the
tighter
it shrank, shaking and
bobbing, but after the wind
calmed widened airy with radiality:
but yesterday late
I blew one time hard on it and it
spilled spooling to the ground:
fine beads, the babies stirred,
cleaning themselves up in
reverse web-flow: one bead
went off a way on a haywire web
but, back to mainline, came
stringing up, the final bead:
dark tightens the ball hard.

Easter Morning

I have a life that did not become,
that turned aside and stopped,
astonished:
I hold it in me like a pregnancy or
as on my lap a child
not to grow or grow old but dwell on

it is to his grave I most
frequently return and return
to ask what is wrong, what was
wrong, to see it all by
the light of a different necessity
but the grave will not heal
and the child,
stirring, must share my grave
with me, an old man having
gotten by on what was left

when I go back to my home country in these
fresh far-away days, it's convenient to visit
everybody, aunts and uncles, those who used to say,
look how he's shooting up, and the
trinket aunts who always had a little
something in their pocketbooks, cinnamon bark
or a penny or nickel, and uncles who

were the rumored fathers of cousins
who whispered of them as of great, if
troubled, presences, and school
teachers, just about everybody older
(and some younger) collected in one place
waiting, particularly, but not for
me, mother and father there, too, and others
close, close as burrowing
under skin, all in the graveyard
assembled, done for, the world they
used to wield, have trouble and joy
in, gone

the child in me that could not become
was not ready for others to go,
to go on into change, blessings and
horrors, but stands there by the road
where the mishap occurred, crying out for
help, come and fix this or we
can't get by, but the great ones who
were to return, they could not or did
not hear and went on in a flurry and
now, I say in the graveyard, here
lies the flurry, now it can't come
back with help or helpful asides, now
we all buy the bitter
incompletions, pick up the knots of
horror, silently raving, and go on
crashing into empty ends not
completions, not rondures the fullness
has come into and spent itself from

I stand on the stump
of a child, whether myself
or my little brother who died, and
yell as far as I can, I cannot leave this place, for
for me it is the dearest and the worst,
it is life nearest to life which is
life lost: it is my place where
I must stand and fail,
calling attention with tears
to the branches not lofting
boughs into space, to the barren
air that holds the world that was my world

though the incompletions
(& completions) burn out
standing in the flash high-burn
momentary structure of ash, still it
is a picture-book, letter-perfect
Easter morning: I have been for a
walk: the wind is tranquil: the brook
works without flashing in an abundant
tranquility: the birds are lively with
voice: I saw something I had
never seen before: two great birds,
maybe eagles, blackwinged, whitenecked
and -headed, came from the south oaring
the great wings steadily; they went
directly over me, high up, and kept on
due north: but then one bird,
the one behind, veered a little to the
left and the other bird kept on seeming

not to notice for a minute: the first
began to circle as if looking for
something, coasting, resting its wings
on the down side of some of the circles:
the other bird came back and they both
circled, looking perhaps for a draft;
they turned a few more times, possibly
rising—at least, clearly resting—
then flew on falling into distance till
they broke across the local bush and
trees: it was a sight of bountiful
majesty and integrity: the having
patterns and routes, breaking
from them to explore other patterns or
better ways to routes, and then the
return: a dance sacred as the sap in
the trees, permanent in its descriptions
as the ripples round the brook's
ripplestone: fresh as this particular
flood of burn breaking across us now
from the sun.

White Dwarf

As I grow older
arcs swollen inside
now and then fall
back, collapsing, into
forming walls:
the temperature shoots
up with what I am not
and am: from
multiplicities, dark
knots, twanging twists,
structures come into sight,
chief of these
a blade of fire only now
so late, so sharp and standing,
burning confusion up.

Distraction

During my glorious,
crazy years, I
went about the business of
the universe relentlessly,
inquired of goat
and zygote,
frill and floss,
touched, tasted,
prodded, and tested and as
it were kept the
whole thing going
by
central attention's
central node:

now my anklebones hurt
when I stand up
or the mail truck
drops by to bury
me under two
small obligations: I
can't quite remember
what call I went to find
or why so much
fell to me: in fact,

sometimes
a whole green sunset
will wash dark
as if it could go
right by without me.

Rapids

Fall's leaves are redder than
spring's flowers, have no pollen,
and also sometimes fly, as the wind
schools them out or down in shoals
or droves: though I
have not been here long, I can
look up at the sky at night and tell
how things are likely to go for
the next hundred million years:
the universe will probably not find
a way to vanish nor I
in all that time reappear.

Neighbors

How little I have really cared about nature: I always
thought the woods idyllic and let it go at that: but,
look, one tree, the near pine, cracked off in high wind,

dry rot at the ground, and coming down sheared every
branch off one side of the sweetgum: one tree, trying
to come up under another, has only one bough in light:

an ice storm some years ago broke the tops off several
trees that now splinter into sprouts: one sweetgum,
bent over bow-like to the ground, has given up its

top and let an arrow of itself rise midway: ivy has
made Ann Pollard's pine an ivy tree: I can't regain
the lost idyllic at all, but the woods are here with us.

Keepsake

I feel the brook as it were
teased and betrayed me, its
finery of glitter enchanting
my mind and leading me off

and off again down the accurate
indifferences of mechanical
shift and spill, inexhaustible
burn of glint and glide: oh,

for when I could give no more
attention up and needed to be
looked for, the brook kept
its old lessons tucked away

as usual in its flowings and
answered only as I guessed it:
but you, lover, prowled the world
to be found and, found, found me:

if you part your lips, the
shifts and spills in your
eyes will break me open: this
lost, I'm unlost and unbetrayed.

Antithesis

If no material and no resort
will hold us in place,
placate and pacify us,

then we have to make up
something out of nothing
(a pliable material) and

loft it (it is not heavy)
high enough to reach beyond
the highest branch we could

pull down, and we have to make it
of perfect understanding
(know-it-all silence) and

able to respond in the fullest
measure (the other side of
emptiness, the broadest

welcome): where can
dense, straw-strung flesh
cry to for its essential

answering other except beyond,
way, way beyond the star
points resolving into galaxies.

Traveling Shows

I found vision and it
was terrific, the sight
enabling and abiding, but
I couldn't get these
old bones there and light's
a byproduct of
rapid decomposition:
I found power, too, but
sick, meal-swollen children
refused it:
no one breathes the held
air in words' winds:
more than could be
promised, the many
graces of accurate
turnings, or even thought
to seek, I found, I
found: it was nothing:
the ghost of the made
world, leaving, enters
the real—no, not that much:
the real world
succeeds the made and,
burnt out, shuts down.

Breaking Out

I have let all my balloons aloose
what will become of them now
pricked they will show some weight
or caught under a cloud lack
ebullience to feel through

but they are all let loose
yellow, red, blue, thin-skinned, tough
and let go they have put me down
I was an earth thing all along
my feet are catching in the brush

Range

In the storm window's upper left
hand corner, between the panes,
a tiny spider angles to catch one
of two fall flies thrice his size:
the flies, addled, sidle about,
over and away, and buzz loose
confined between the windows and
bowl over into the corner occasionally,
snapping webs, guy wires, cross
references: the predator feints
at the fly-throughs and, missing,
sits before diving to re-build:
it tests patience when what you need
is too big to handle: but the flies
may weaken and wander where the weakest
web can hold down one of their
few possibilities left,
while the fine spider may go on
living on air if need be till this plenty.

Dry Spell Spiel

It's so far to the brook the squirrel
nips dew off the garage roof
dipping down from tile tip to tip,
stopping head sideways and one paw up in still

perception (fear) then melting
into motion and need: this is another
day, high blue, that won't leave
drop or dampening anywhere

by noon: even the brook way off
trickles clinging to the ledges: how many
territories are riddled with routes, easements
to the brook banks, as grackles, robins,

catbirds get through: the snake lies
all the way long in and dimples
the transparence with the brilliant
surfacing of two diamond nostrils, needlepoints

that give the whole length air: the
pheasant keeps to underbrush on his way:
a salamander is sticking with the wet
leaves under my leaky outdoor faucet.

Mountain Wind

I went out into the cancellations of the wind
and stood still
my arms up stiff
like shrubs

Oh I said I have discovered my consequence
This celebration of
water and lust is not
my celebration but a speech

the deep says and sends the wind through
I touched the sharp tips
of stalks and stood in the lone
hurry of time down the mountain slope

Night Finding

Open and naked under the big snow
the hill cemetery by the falls
looks felled to stump stone

and the rich spray of the summer
falls gathers absent into
glazes of ice wall: here in the

backyard thicket sway-floats
of honeysucklebush brush
(once misted berry red)

bend down to solid touch,
and weed clumps break off
into halfway teepees:

pheasant in the earliest pearl
of dusk bluster in, swirls of
landing and looking, and settled

to the dusk mode, walk under
the snow slants and shelters easing
through brush fox would noticeably jar.

Fourth Dimension

Reason can't end:
it is discourse, motion
to find motion, reason to
find reason to abandon
reason: when the argument
no longer thruways, the
road closes: poetry can
come complete, take on
shape, end into
winding up itself, any
violation of which
totally violating:
the shape does not depend
elsewhere to make itself
felt: it is as
it is: it can't be cast
aside except to cast that
shape aside, no part in it
free to cast free any
part: improved, it
concludes in dust,
an end both as
itself and not as itself.

Country Music

Snow melt and flood
rushes finished, the
brook evens down to

groundwater—black
clarity, water glass,
of the central bed

bending white spill-arc
hooks over the ledge!
oh, the lolling, timeless

music, inharmony so
various it finds harmony's
underlying mix: but

the next stepledge
upstream sends down
high, thin, hushed

tones, an obbligato,
the far range filtered
free to a band of drowse.

Wiring

Radiance comes from
on high and, staying,
sends down silk
lines to the flopping
marionette, me, but
love comes from
under the ruins and
sends the lumber up
limber into leaf that
touches so high it nearly
puts out the radiance

Sunday at McDonald's

In the bleak land of foreverness no
one lives but only, crushed and buffeted,
now: now, now, now every star glints

perishing while now slides under and
away, slippery as light, time-vapor:
what can butterflies do or clear-eyed

babies gumming french fries—nature
is holding them, somehow, veering them
off into growth holdings, forms

brought to peaks of splendor, sharp
energies burring into each other to
set off new progressions through the

rustle and mix, rot and slush: is
this the way it is: sometimes a man
will stand up, clear and settled as

a bright day, and seem to look through
the longest times and roilings to
the still, star-bending, fixed ahead.

Sweetened Change

The small white-headed man pops out
his side and begins the ten-minute
procedure of getting her out the car:
he unloads the wheelchair first:
the wife, snow white, gets turned
around, the toes so carefully tender
and tended, till she sits looking as
if headed sideways: she finds in herself
weight's structure and, rising, falls
translated to the wheels: such
satisfaction and relief! but, now, the
leg must be elevated, billows and strings,
and special consideration given the spine's
new crimp: it all works out, some
tucking in and looking around: off they roll
through the hospital doors: soon the quick
man is out again, squeals away to parking
spaces allotted longer stalls of time:
he jogs back by and back through the doors
he goes: one mate gives out and the other
buzzes fast to sing he's not alone and idle.

Parting

She was already lean when
a stroke or two slapped
her face like drawn
claw prints: akilter, she
ate less and

sat too much on the edge
of beds looking a width too
wide out of windows:
she lessened: getting
out for a good day, she sat

on the bench still and
thin as a porch post:
the children are all
off, she would think, but a
minute later,

startle, where are the children,
as if school had let
out: her husband watched
her till loosened away himself
for care: then,

seeming to know but never
quite sure, she was put in
a slightly less hopeful
setting: she watched her
husband tremble in to call

and shoot up high head-bent
eyes: her mind
flashed clear through, she was
sure of it, she had seen
that one before: her husband

longed to say goodbye or else
hello, but the room stiffened
as if two lovers had just caught
on sight, every move rigid
misfire in that perilous fire.

Feel Like
Traveling On

Sit down and be patient:
sure, it's a beautiful,
endless, lonely Sunday
afternoon: the old people
are in their graves:
the old places are deserted:
the times of all those
times, faces, flavors
a few minds left hold:
sure, ahead the chief
business is tearing the rest
of the way loose: but by
the empty take the full:
sit down, find something
to read: a grand possibility
was made: who knows
what became of it

Poverty

I'm walking home from, what,
a thousandth walk this year
along the same macadam's edge
(pebbly) the ragweed rank
but not blooming yet,
a rose cloud passed to the
east that against sundown would be
blue-gray, the moon up nearly
full, splintering
through the tips of street pine,
and the hermit lark downhill
in a long glade cutting
spirals of musical ice, and I
realize that it is not the same for
me as for others, that
being here to be here
with others is for others.

Givings

Why not let the name go with the body
since things will be
as they appear

a shambles of change with now and then an absolute
loss and most changes, re-directions not
the kind you can bend back into shape

and not even in the midridge of the overspill
an island to stop on and consider in stillness time
passing

but only in the interweavings, flows back and
forth, under and over, around and through
does reality hold

to a single face its name and that can
on a stormy spring morning seem so underbuilt
with dream, reality & appearance flow together away

An Improvisation for
the Stately Dwelling

This fall morning is pretty much
like a fall morning
                the bottoms of poplars
and tops of beeches
leafless
    a wind NNW
    has re-lifted the geese
    and sent them southerly
    I know a man whose cancer has
    got him just to the point
    he looks changed by a flight of stairs
people pass him and speak
extra-brightly
he asks nothing else
he is like a rock
reversed, that is, the rock has a solid
body and shakes only
reflected in the water but he shakes
in body only,
his spirit a boulder of light
    nature
    includes too much

and art can't include enough
the sky is soft this morning
all gray,
regioned here and there with ivory
light
the flames of climbing vines are
shedding out, falling back,
stringing fire
the brook almost blisters with
cool equations among the fallen colors
what is to become of us we know
how are we to be taken by it or take it

An Improvisation
for Jerald Bullis

It's not much of a fall with
hemlocks

    the new green already
advanced,
needles inwardly hidden
turn brown
and make not much of shedding

        catch the right
        windy day to catch
        the show right

one day in a high wind,
every ready needle already
gone, nothing
will fall
though the billows of boughs
    heave and slosh
    but another day after a
    calm
    the needles wait in a small wind
    for the windtwist to reap them,
    a bunch, salience, weave, or warp
    of them coming down

              spinning or
              striking boughs and, whooshed up,
              spinning again
till
on the ground
a fairly unnoticeable, diffuse
browning
comes over things,
particular needles subsumed and
nothing outlined

                    so many falls all summer and
                    even earlier in earliest spring and
                    later falls than fall, wild carrot
                    seeds held in ribbed cups
                    sprinkling out over ice

the speaker, delivered out of himself,
places his "I"
anywhere
in rose or rat
and feels the speech he has deserved to
say,
himself so much given over, unfolded, that he
is mostly without interest

light fills volumes
shade clears

the big garden spider sits in air between
the two hedge headlands and doesn't move
enough to close down for dusk

Persistences

Wind, though in the temple,
criticizes the pillars,
from bronze walls and set
floors
takes haze away, a small
flour
given back to the desert:
nuzzles into alcoves and porticoes
as if glad to
take on the curvature

and drowse
but leaks and brushes away again
restless with what
remains a while:
the theorem of the wind
no pigment, wall, or word
disproves: propositions
scatter before it,
grow up in brier thickets
and thistle thickets:

still, from our own ruins,
we thrash out the
snakes and mice,
shoo the lean ass away,
and plant a row of something:
we know,
we say to the wind, but we will
come back again and back:
in debris we make a holding as
insubstantial and permanent as mirage.